The
Journey with
Nature Continues

Gary Frederic

Published 2024
Printed in the United States of America

First Edition
ISBN (print): 978-1-963380-16-3
ISBN (e-book): 978-1-963380-17-0

For information, address:
Holzer Books LLC
8 The Green, Ste. A
Dover, Delaware 19901 USA

For information about special discounts available for bulk purchases, sales promotions, and educational needs, contact:
info@holzerbooksllc.com
+1 (888) 901-7776

Scripture quotations are taken from the New World Translation of The Holy Scriptures (2013 Revision), published by Jehovah's Witnesses.

Cover art background designed by asrulaqroni - Freepik.com

holzerbooksLLC©

TABLE OF CONTENTS

Adrift Comes Snow

In the clouds above,
you sit concealed with doves.
As you await your chariots to freeze,
to send you to your new home by a breeze.
O beautiful snow,
the wonders you intend to show!
You force us – every work to stop.
Even travelers you mock.
You tell us all to make the Winter bed,
by making our light red.
While you are given the greenlight to go,
adrift comes snow!
You ask us to ponder,
because it will make the heart fonder.
Just thank God that he made her!
The clouds are in labor.

Big-up To Europe

List the gist
Linguist to assist
Name the game
Plane to Spain
Deplane to train
Amid Madrid
Corona in Barcelona
Not to embarrass
Kiss to Paris
Dance in France
Turn to Lucerne
Swiss I miss
This was bliss
Little-we in Italy
Roam in Rome
Whisk to brisk
Swish to British
Spend with friends
Overspending ends
Home to moan
Big-up to Europe

Don't Leave This Classroom

You may have graduated high school,
but only this training will give you the best tools!
Class has just begun;
and it's really going to be fun!
Jehovah's the one with the pen;
and the Benefits from His instruction has no end.
They come from two different books.
The first is the book of creation;
it's a book made to fill the heart with appreciation!
The second is His written Word, the Bible.
These writings live and are not idle.
Don't leave this classroom,
because these instructions will forever feed your interior room!
Class is in session,
and this teacher is fun!
Giving practical lessons;
He doesn't bore anyone!
Who needs to hear a bell?
In this class the heart swells.
Just don't leave this classroom.

Earth is a Living Museum

Our home is a living museum
In each display you can clearly see Him
On display are art, culture, history and science
Like the laws of gravity, they benefit all in compliance

All these collections were made to exhibit His personality
They were made for all people — no matter what the nationality
Study them
In each one you'll find Him

You can tell this One is a perfect host
Confidently in Him we can boast
Even the air we breathe is free
Although others try to make us pay a fee

Make Him the one you admire most
For his artistry and creativity, it's **Jehovah** we must promote
Search for that warm feeling inside
Study His works and enjoy the ride

He *truly* is the *Greatest Of All Time*
Because no other like Him can create
"The works of Jehovah are great;
They are studied by all those finding pleasure in them" – Psalms 111:2.
Because all his works truly are the crème de la crème

Dragons Tamed By Butterflies

You are a smiling sea monster,
with armor that is hard to pierce.
Your teeth look like the tips of spears.
What dentist can say: 'Open your mouth wide while I examine.'
What hygienist can clean your teeth?
Although you never frown, and are always smiling,
you are still not approachable!
Who would try getting next to you?
There's only one who can stand up to you eye to eye...
Yes, one that would win you over.
It doesn't need to pierce your armor,
nor does it need to hold down your mouth.
All it does is land on your sensitive eyes,
to use its gentle tongue to dry your tears.
Who knew a mighty dragon could be tamed by a butterfly?

How true these words: "*A gentle tongue can break a bone.*"
– Proverbs 25:15.

Escort

Because you did not need a passport,
I crossed every border with you as my escort.
No matter what country we were in,
you were the perfect blend!
We sat together at cafés;
and some mornings we ate together at the bays.
Although we landed together in Spain,
at times we flew together without being on an airplane.
All my trips with you made me feel at home.
You were the best linguist, especially in Paris and Rome!
The experience we brewed was exuberant.
Our taste buds talked together with humor and...
You percolated through me with flavor;
memories of our trips together we still savor.
Even when down under, though not an Aussie,
my escort – Coffee.

Forever Amber

She's easy to love,
Uniquely mild,
A glamourous burst,
My thirst endowed,
A yellow rose,
With charms of sent,
For the nose amend,
Her heart is a pendant,
A course of brilliance,
Commends the earth,
Shows much resilience,
Though trials contend,
With adulation,
Great Melody,
For Jah she brings,
And Spring endears,
A time of rise,
Like joy of Summer,
A star aglow,
Cause hearts to melt,
Like dazzling blossoms,
A sight enjoyed,
Employed like rainbow,
Her color joys,
A moon astounds,
Sound is mine,
A June of bliss,
A beauty enshrined,
An amber of rich!

Giraffe

With so little sleep
A big heart beat
And extremely high blood pressure
A very tall stature — with many pounds to measure
The flow of your arteries must be demanding
How in the world do you keep standing
You're not faking it
You can really take a hit
Out here you don't need to duck
Really, you do stand up
To see your towering neck
We've made this trek
To see your striking long legs
We spent our nest egg
Giraffe
At the man on stilts you laugh
The One who made your heart this stable
Can surely make all our anxieties disable
Especially when in worry and I'm in want to dash
Let joy dive into my heart and cause a splash
Let me laugh
Let my heart beat like the Giraffe

I Speak More When I Can't Sleep

Tonight, you are alluring
You have taken away my dream of deep
Because my heart needs curing
Now I can't sleep

I would tell you to bother the moon
Because it is nocturnal
But stay; when you leave I'll just sleep till noon
Now I want to read you my journal

Let the fireflies take over tonight
Because they speak this same message
For they also because of love ignite
I need help with this wreckage

We have an Orchestra with background music — the crickets
If I let this night go I'd miss it
So, let's talk
Please, take notes
Use the night sky as your board and the moon as your chalk
Because I still have hopes

I'd Dry Up

I'm just a puddle;
you're an ocean.
People love to visit and travel with you!
They just cross over me.
You even fight back when the storms hit you.
I'd dry up.
The Sun and Moon loves standing with you,
But I'd dry up.
Even the ponds — when they freeze from cold
— come back; and life within, they still hold.
Like frost I would melt in the heat;
And I would drop like a tear does.
I'd still smile, though,
because I would not escape His notice.
I'd be a tear He'd remember.
Although I'm none of these aquatic places that are captivating,
He'd remember me, because I dried up for Him.

I Tire Not To Tire Out

On this journey there's many obstacles;
one wrong turn can lead you to the hospital.
I tire not to tire out;
But this is definitely the best route!
My mind sees for my heart.
For checkout, your words have been put in my cart.
My very bones and my sinews;
these also want to feel you.
This is no easy task!
That's why I tirelessly ask.
Because I don't want to live wrong,
my heart keeps crying: *'Hold on!'*
I tire not to tire out;
but I have to win this bout.

I'm Sticking to You Like Glue!

With you, my home is already made.
"When I'm afraid,
I put my trust in you." – Psalm 56:3.
I'm sticking to you like glue!
When I'm in your care,
there are no worries on which to stare.
Whether I'm in the open or enclosed,
under your hand there is no threat imposed.
I am in no want nor in any need to attain,
because my rest and movements reside in your domain.
There's no weather too cold,
nor any hand greater than yours to hold.
I know that you're a fortress around;
for in you, I feel a power and force which surrounds!
My sleep is always pleasant and secure,
because I have a great comforter which is sure.
What greater arms can hold me?
For there is no one that outstretches your hand;
and there's no one against you to withstand!
Even if my eyes should close,
and the air flow would stop to pass through my nose;
I know that you can re-open my eyes,
and cause air once again to filtrate inside.
"I put my trust in you!"
And, I'm sticking to you like glue!

Kanga Who?

These should be called Australia's deer
They bounce everywhere
I'm really down under
Kangaroos are just one of your many wonders
Even the Joey is carried close to their core
They don't run on all four
They all hop on two
Kangaroo
I bet they can strike faster than Ali
Please! Don't strike me
It looks like a boxer on springs
They should sing: *'Fly like a butterfly and like a bee stings'*
Kangaroo
Their feet make them look like they're experts in Kung Fu
So, at the end of the day
They have many things to display
For now, we've made a pactum
Since we have much to learn about them
I'd say: *'Kanga who?'*
Because I think we don't have a clue

Like a Golden Eagle

Your splendor is seen from your golden crown!
With wings like an eagle you soar down;
and like a storm wind your answers come.
The food you give is generous and without sum.
Swiftly soaring — you zoom down from the sky with your keen sight.
And with mighty talons you always stand for what is right.
From where you can see everything – above the clouds – sits your mound.
Like a flash of light and a rushing sound,
you swoop down to pilot your young.
Their cries are precious to you; yes, all of them are heard like music sung.
To lead and teach your hatchlings the right thing,
with your powerful beak your sayings come down like lightning.
And to comfort those in your nest,
your eyes are fixed upon your belongings to give them rest.
You also spread your wings over us,
so that no harm may come, nor any predator to cause a fuss.
Yes, because of the covenant you have with your people,
to harm us will always be illegal.
That is why we can forever say: 'Study them; because they remind me of him!'
For it is written: *"Just as an eagle stirs up its nest, Hovers over its fledglings, Spreading out its wings, taking them, Carrying them on its pinions, Jehovah alone kept leading him"*. - Deuteronomy 32:11-12.

Miss Alps

I saw your smile
From peak to peak stretching for miles
It was wide and picturesque
I couldn't believe it
I had to give my eyes a recheck
This is a place where people faint in
You looked like a painting
For the moon you were a candle stand
And for the sun a lampstand
Your presence was so calming
I was in a place that could make you Psalms sing
The clouds wrapped around you like a shawl
Just laying eyes on you was a gift in all
Switzerland
The paradise I was in

My Compass

You know that I like to travel;
but I don't always know my way.
Like the pointer in a compass,
no matter where I go,
may my heart always point back towards you.

Then, even when I'm disoriented
and don't know my way,
with you – I will never be lost!

Whether traveling on a straight line
or making circles;
like a compass, may my heart always point to you.

Red Rose

As the morning glory shines to reveal her magnificent form, her petals hint a ruby. Her oil descends and frames her like golden honey. Her pleasant aroma becomes entwined with the atmosphere that surrounds her. Intrigued and fascinated by her splendor, eyes have become alert. This is truly a rose. It doesn't just speak to the eyes; it resonates deep down to what is enclosed!

Our Superstar

Your cheerleaders – the birds – rise up before you do!
To introduce and welcome you they're singing;
like little alarm clocks they're ringing!

The champ is about to wake up.
Even oceans and seas are running to fill its cup.

It's chasing the moon away!
Like a king it rules the day.

When the Sun opens it eye,
the clouds look like floating cotton candy.
Its glory shines on everything we see!

So that we may carry out our work with smiles,
the sun's rays will be seen for miles

With your lasso you keep our home in your orbit.
To keep us cheerful, playing with the other stars you forfeit

Our daystar
This is earth's superstar

She's a Swan — Give Her The Moon, Not Pearls

Never give a pearl to a Swan,
because the Moon is better.
She is already beautiful;
so, give her something that will make
her feel beautiful within.
Make her feel like she's on top of your world.

You love her, right?
Then give her something else that is not common;
everyone gives Pearls.
Think big; think outside of this world.

Give her the moon – it's evocative.
True, you could never make that happen;
but work hard to get it as if it's already hers.
It would remind her that you
will always try to give her your best.

She will never forget it;
because the moon is better than pearls.
And she *is* really worth it!

GARY FREDERIC

Something Better Than Balsam From Gilead

Something special has been arranged for you!
It was a costly cure;
but it will make you new.
Your price — just to endure.
It will make you fresher than your youth.
For shade and protection from storms,
it will be your booth.
From aches and pains it transforms.
Something better than the balsam from Gilead;
it will reverse the effects of what all illness did!
And the most valuable thing ever?
Your benefits will last forever!

Surf the Turf

By the coastline,
I can taste the *real* surf and turf.
What a marvel of design!
Although I wish to roam the earth,
I also want to make the ocean my turf.
I enjoy this song it plays,
because it holds its notes for endless days.
When the Sun surfs on you,
you come alive and you're new.
You're happy, because I can see you foam.
This is the best time to roam!
Surf the turf;
then you'll truly appreciate its worth!

The More I Travel

The more I travel, the more I see the earth so great
I can see the beauty of a world aged with grace
We are all contributions created to participate
Made to give no matter what color the face

The majority of the pursuits in this life are fleeting
They are all nothing but a false dream
Things that at the end truly make the heart stop beating
But there's so much — though different — that can unite us as a team

We thrive on the same things, though grown on different soils
Our needs are satisfied by the same sun and water
We benefit and are nourished by the same oils
If we all saw it the same way, we'd never each other slaughter

The more I travel, I can see that we're really all together in it
We can't stop time, nor turn back the numbers
We have so much to lose and need every minute
There's a sleep that wants to arrest us — greater than slumber

Whether by air, sea or on the ground
The more I travel, I long for another tomorrow
Because exploring gives ecstatic feelings that are profound
These naturally take away what causes sorrow

The Resplendent Island

We were sent to serve you with encouragement;
but you served us with nourishment.
With your greeting: 'Ayubowan',
you already had our hearts won!
It was love that made us bind.
We will forever have you on our mind.
You lost sleep for us;
for this we give you a plus.
Your people are so beautiful!
You gave us something new that rose to the full.
The Resplendent Island;
a place we traveled many a mile and...
Where many were made feeble;
We love your people!
Everything from Ceylon tea,
and the delicious things from the Indian Sea.
Lagoon Crabs and spices,
with the sides the knife dices;
you can curry me up anytime!
It was worth every nickel, every dime.
We enjoyed it all!
To be honest, for **Sri Lanka**, the heart still calls.
Because you truly are a Resplendent Island.

Ayubowan /eye-bow-one/:
A Sri Lankan greeting that means 'Long live' or 'Long life'.

The Rambutan

This fruit with spikes
Just wanted my taste buds to strike
If you didn't see anyone collect it
It'd be a fruit that's deceptive
You don't want to hurt me
With a core that is sweet
You just wanted to take me off my feet
No more uhm...
This is like rum
Now I desire to get into your interior room
Because I've tasted you without your costume

The Trumpet That Truly Praises You

Because of your connections
you stand tall;
and you toot your horn!
Your muscles you flex.
And although you have none,
you can break bones.
Your lips can lift me up.
You're a flexible hose that refreshes.
With all the work you do,
your trumpet truly praises Him!
If my lips worked like you,
I'd be in the Guinness book of world records.
Unfortunately, though,
my lips hit harder than yours;
yes, mine can break the soul.
So, I must continue learning from you;
because your trumpet truly praises Him.
Powerful, yet lifting;
strong, yet gentle.
Your trumpet truly praises Him!

Walk With Me Into Paradise

The breath of life He gives
That we might have this happy life and live
Let us walk together and pray
And enjoy the wonders of this day
Talk to me like lovers do
Walk with me into paradise and let's enjoy the view
As we watch the sun set
Pondering together on the day we met
As we glance at the appearance of the moon
Looking to future blessings that will come soon

We Saw The Moon In Paris

It sat on the Eiffel tower while we visited there
It invited us up for a tour
But all we could do was stare
It gave our hearts a wonderful décor
In the city of romance
Even Cafés were in a trance
I'm just glad that we don't have to Imagine
We saw and felt the passion
I'm going to give you a quiz
Can anyone declare you as his
What fashion model can share this
We saw the moon in Paris
It sat in the city of romance
To let us know that it will always have the last dance
We know and can bear witness
No matter where we travel, every heart is on its hit list
We saw the moon in Paris
Ah, that we also miss

Why The Oceans Have More Tears Than Us

You have endurance,
because you are determined to keep trying;
and while trying you endure storms.
You're even beaten by the wind.
But while you're moving forward
and enduring all of this,
you're also helping others to travel.
And what you have stored within, you generously share!
Now we know that you cry because you're happy.
When we see and experience moments with you,
although your tears are so many,
we know that you are happy.
This is why the oceans have more tears than us;
they are helping others while enduring their race!

www.ingramcontent.com/pod-product-compliance
Lightning Source LLC
Chambersburg PA
CBHW031300120626
46545CB00007B/2908